1·45

D1426506

WITHDRAWN FROM
THE LIBRARY

UNIVERSITY OF
WINCHESTER

KA 0030331 3

Railway Architecture of the South-East

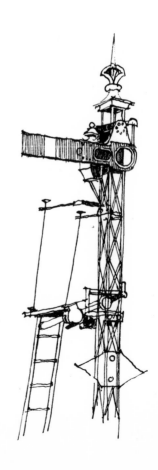

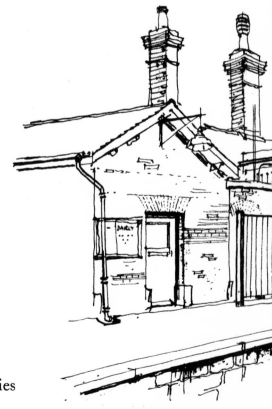

Railway Architecture Series

Railway Architecture of the South-East

Rodney Symes & David Cole

OSPREY

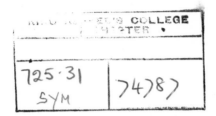

COLLEGE

725·31
SYM   74787

Published in England by

Osprey Publishing Ltd.,
707 Oxford Road, Reading, Berkshire
© Copyright 1972 Osprey Publishing Ltd.
All rights reserved

SBN 85045 070 5

Printed in Great Britain by
The Berkshire Printing Co. Ltd., Reading

Contents

Introduction

The South-East of England (which for this purpose excludes
London but includes Kent, Surrey, Sussex and Hampshire)
covers the area served by the former London Chatham
& Dover and South-Eastern Railways which joined forces
in 1900; by the well-loved London Brighton & South Coast
Railway; and, in part, that of the London & South-Western
Railway. These three lines in 1923 became the Southern
Railway. Some lines of the former Great Western Railway
penetrated the geographical South-East, but as this railway,
with its personal traditions and practices, is so associated
with the South-West, it seems wisest to exclude it from the
South-East. In addition there were several minor railways,
but however fascinating from a locomotive point of view,
they were architecturally negligible. All the railways in the
area, of course, became part of British Railways in 1948.

Now a few words on the scope of railway architecture.
The most prominent examples are of course the stations,
a specialised form of building varying immensely in size
though with certain functional requirements: but there are
also railwaymen's and crossing keepers' cottages, goods sheds
and engine sheds, water-tanks, signal boxes, and engineering
works such as bridges, viaducts and especially tunnel-mouths.
Notable also are such installations as platelayers' huts,
signals, and notices, and near-railway architecture such as
rail-side industry and public houses, or railway-owned docks.
On the other hand, railway-managed hotels have generally
been ignored.

It is natural that many buildings and installations, especially the smaller items, should have been the subject of standardization plans over the years, but variety occurs due to the supplanting of one standard by another, perhaps due to technical reasons, and to the 'one-off' rebuilding to which the South-East, an area of great rail traffic growth in more recent times, has been unusually susceptible. The impact of standard details of one period on a standard of another interested us a great deal: a mid-Victorian building, cleansed of its advertisements and with modern lettering and lighting, may look better than it ever did before. But—and architecturally it is quite important—a number of lines were commenced or built by a local company which soon sold out to one of the larger lines, like the Margate Railway, on which Birchington was situated, which in 1863 was opened under Chatham & Dover auspices.

A feature of all railway buildings after the very earliest period is the use of alien materials—Welsh slate, red bricks from the Midlands, Gault bricks from Suffolk, and much else. This is of course not confined to railway buildings, but shows how railways transformed the transport of heavy goods, especially in an area like the Weald, where the heavy clay could seriously impede road transport for half the year. Welsh slates and Midland bricks together with Durham coal could now very readily and speedily reach the towns and country railheads, and with notable effect. Take for example Crowborough, where the local brick, of which most buildings for some distance round are built, is manufactured a stone's throw from the station. The latter when rebuilt in the late 'nineties was not in the local brick because something harder was required and it was easily brought to the site.

Railways began seriously in the South-East around 1840, and, perhaps because the considerable opposition to this innovation required a certain amount of care in image-projection, the four main companies (or their predecessors) all started by using architects to design at any rate their major buildings. The London & South-Western used William Tite

(1798–1873, and later in life Sir William Tite, M.P.), a successor of Sir John Soane at one remove and a considerable architect of railway stations. He produced classic revival designs of much charm, like Southampton Terminus (and perhaps also Gosport). The Brighton had its earliest stations and structures designed by David Mocatta, a pupil of Soane, but most of his station work has been swept away or built round. The Chatham & Dover was only opened in 1858 and so missed this period entirely. The South-Eastern patronized Samuel Beazley (1786–1851), who is one of those strange figures, once well thought of and now quite neglected: he lived at Tonbridge Castle and at Soho Square, wrote operas and farces, and specialized in theatres; but it is difficult to pin down any remains of his station work with certainty—perhaps the picturesque 'Tudor' at Grove·Ferry, so like many other stations of the time, or the severe Doric at Canterbury West.

The 'Railway Mania' of 1846, when railway promotion and speculation got entirely out of hand, was followed by a sharp reaction in the following years, and this led to architects being dispensed with as a luxury. Many of the technical problems had been worked out, so builders got on with the minor works and engineers with the major. In this period each line, as opened, would typically have a more or less standard station repeated along it, with the major traffic centres being 'one-off' due to the needs of their traffic and layout but incorporating no doubt standard elements. Sometimes this was less than perfect: the Brighton, after a number of charming cottages like those along the west coast line, of which Yapton is an example, that owed something to Mocatta, settled for a plain T-shaped effort rendered dirty grey, which had larger variants, like Kemp Town (1869) with a few classic details added, varied by sundry structures in a debased Georgian, like Pulborough (1862), and others with vaguely Gothic detail, of which Buxted (1864) may serve as an example, the Gothic revival having during this second period become established as a proper 'style' for secular buildings under the earnest influence of such architects as George Gilbert Scott and William Butterfield in their respective manners. The South-Eastern and South-Western had little consistency, favouring adaptations of whatever villas were locally being built, with added, as it were, outbuildings. The Chatham & Dover, always an impecunious line due to its obsessive competition with the South-Eastern, nevertheless had unpretentious, pleasant, light brick buildings, of which Sole Street is a good example, on the lines between St Mary Cray and Strood, and between Faversham and Dover, built around 1860.

The 'fifties may perhaps be described as an era of 'growing pains', financially, mechanically and operationally, whilst the early 'sixties were a time of financial troubles marked by several spectacular bankruptcies of railway contractors of the standing of Grissell and Peto (who built railways in North Kent). But by the late 'sixties things were looking up. For instance, the Brighton Railway's locomotive 'new look' of the eighteen-seventies and its improved prosperity after the financial straits of the eighteen-sixties which led, in this particular case, to the abandonment of works already started, are paralleled by its buildings, for there emerges a consistent style, a free 'Gothic' of which good examples are at Box Hill, Leatherhead, Lewes and Eastbourne. Box Hill (1877) is one of a series by the architect C. H. Driver (1832–1900) which have picturesque roof lines and small towers; Eastbourne has a tower and a high roof with a lantern over the booking hall; Lewes (1889) has a sort of screen wall with large balls on the parapet and another form of lantern. Tunbridge Wells West, of the eighteen-eighties, on the other hand, looks like the work of an engineer who had seen illustrations of the nineteenth-century architect William Butterfield's buildings: it too has a high clock tower (and a lantern over the loo), but it is interesting also in that, save for the demise of steam, time has stood still for at least forty years and probably much longer, so that it is rather a good museum of the sort of Victorian details British Rail are only too anxious to sweep off the face of the earth. All these Brighton stations must be regarded as in danger at the present time.

Parallel with this there developed another style which derived from the country houses being built in areas of Sussex and Surrey at the time, where red brick and tile were used and details looked backwards to the early eighteenth century—the so-called 'Queen Anne' style developed notably by Norman Shaw and J. J. Stevenson, and which saddened Gilbert Scott so much. Horsted Keynes and Sheffield Park (1882) are examples of this. Crowborough is another 'country house', and design of a high order. Christ's Hospital (1902) needs a mention, not on account of its station house, but because of the high architectural quality of the timber, cast iron and glass platform structures. It is, incidentally, an example of a peculiar Brighton foible, that of building enormous stations in the middle of nowhere, sometimes it is true with horse race traffic in mind. Singleton, Horsted Keynes, Eridge and Lingfield are other examples. Another Brighton characteristic of the time was to lay out an immense forecourt in front of its stations, so that these at any rate have now no car parking problem.

The other railways in the South-East built, let us face it, not very memorable stations in the late nineteenth century, though those like Petersfield on the Portsmouth Direct line of the South-Western, a narrow three-storey gabled house contrasting with single-storey station offices, are striking. Many were engineers' or builders' adaptations of what had gone before, but such, in the verdant countryside, have (or in most cases had) a bucolic charm difficult to pin down on paper, and one day they will be subjected to a specialist study. In any case, the major part of the Dover and South-Eastern systems had been built by 1875 and that of the Brighton by 1885, so that new work usually involved extension and renewal in order to take care of widening or increased traffic. The South-Western, when pressed, used, at the turn of the century, either a variant of the Brighton country house, or a neo-Georgian straight out of Jaggard & Drury's *Building Construction*, like the Railway Orphanage at Woking.

A characteristic of new stations opened after 1900 was that, since they were, unless in suburban locations, catering for places where traffic was slight, they were very economical. To this class belongs, for example, the timber structures on the old Kent & East Sussex Railway, any one of which might have cost as much as fifty pounds new.

The Southern Railway in its new work, of which there was a good deal connected with the widespread electrification schemes, tended to follow the South-Western neo-Georgian, much modified as time went on. Tunbridge Wells Central is a rich example: Haywards Heath of about 1934 is a restrained brick building characteristic of that period. Dumpton Park of 1926, on the other hand, is a rogue building deserving more than a look, and some of the buildings in the railway-owned Southampton Docks are not dissimilar.

There are some post-war examples of note. The Southampton ocean liner terminal building is pompous and unpleasant, but Gatwick, rebuilt in the nineteen-fifties and joined to the glossy air terminal by a covered way, is a fine example of an effort to combine air and rail travel by giving the rail passenger the aseptic environment associated with air travel.

The details other than the buildings, which form part of the composition, such as footbridges, seats, fences, lamps and so on, are important. Footbridges over the line often dominate the station, especially if they are of the not uncommon type with latticed sides and a corrugated steel roof, but they are often timber and glass rather in the style of signal boxes. They may help to unify the composition by holding together the two separate parts of the station, inevitably separate (in the absence of an all over roof or of an island platform) because the lines run through the middle. Fences are of iron, or wooden palings, and are rarely ornamental. The Southern Railway made a great deal of use of standardized pre-cast concrete for such small items as fences, lamp standards, platform edges, platelayers' huts, gradient posts, ballast bins, electric conduit covers and posts— the list is a long one, and examples may be seen everywhere.

Turning now to buildings other than stations. There are four major locomotive or carriage building establishments in the South-East: at Ashford, Brighton, Lancing and Eastleigh. These complexes of factory buildings are by and large of no architectural merit, although the persevering might find items of industrial archaeology which had escaped British Rail's determination to erase its history. Carriage sheds, we find, are usually asbestos-covered industrial buildings. Locomotive sheds, from functional requirements, run to a type. The early examples, either simple buildings with a door at one end and smoke vents in the roof, or 'round houses', either complete or partial, the tracks served from a central turntable, are now very hard to find, but numbers of the larger steam engine sheds, often dating from the later nineteenth century and in effect factory type buildings having roofs with ventilators, either clear span or supported intermediately on rows of columns between the lines, and one end all openings, are still in use as sheds for diesel motive power. The example at Tunbridge Wells is typical: it retains its water-tank and other appurtenances.

Signal boxes are a specialist study. Originally all manually operated, they require a housing for the levers and other apparatus, invariably with a wide and deep window for good visibility up and down the track, usually of timber and usually on the first floor, above a brick or timber base. A stereotyped form in use throughout the country had evolved by the eighteen-eighties, and survived to the nineteen-fifties. There were some notable variants: Cooksbridge is an example of one without a base, and the Brighton at one time used to mount similar boxes on immensely high timber legs: it would also, at country stations, place the apparatus on the station platform. At Petersfield there is a glazed box cantilevered from the station wall. More recently, brick has been used, still with the large windows: a small example is at Grain, at the end of the branch from Gravesend, a long large one at Three Bridges, with wings incorporating sub-stations and so on. The attendant signals come mainly in two sorts. One is the 'semaphore' type with an arm which is raised or lowered, and a lamp with glasses. The post may be timber or steel, latticed or tubular. The other is the 'colour light', which is now usual on heavily-trafficked lines.

Goods sheds have certain precise functional requirements. In them, goods are transhipped under cover between rail and road. A building with doors in one or both ends has inside a platform with perhaps a simple crane, and side doors form a loading bay for road vehicles. A small office is included or attached. They come, of course, in various sizes: within the general pattern, there is a fascinating variety of architectural detail. Once familiar at almost every country station, the concentration of goods traffic at few railheads means that many have lost their use. Perhaps someone will do a detailed study of the type before they all disappear.

Bridges, tunnels, and especially viaducts, are often prominent features in the landscape, and although the South-East is by no means mountainous it has a full share of these engineering features. The scale of some of the earliest viaducts fascinated contemporaries, for they were among the largest civil engineering works of their time, and still impress. Although Mocatta's stations have been altered or destroyed, the Ouse Valley Viaduct of 1840 near Haywards Heath, for which the engineer J. U. Rastrick and he were responsible, remains as his monument, with its piers pierced by elliptical arches and with its ornamental balustrade and end pavilions, whilst later and simpler viaducts, like that between Crowborough and Buxted, have something of the air of a Roman aqueduct. Both of these examples are of brick. The viaduct which carries one of the new lines of 1889 over the old sidings at Lewes, on the other hand, is of steel girders on brick piers. The flyover at Worting Junction on the London & South-Western Railway main line is an example of the noisy latticed steel structure, economising on material rather than on labour, and looking incongruous in its country setting.

Tunnels are of course less prominent because underground, but the round ventilating shafts are a feature of many hills, once steaming but now no longer. Ornamental tunnel mouths are a peculiarly British characteristic. One of the earliest, perhaps in deference to the natural reluctance of early railway travellers to going underground, is the castellated south portal of Clayton Tunnel near Brighton, and Gothic and Classic entrances, of greater or less scholarship, occur throughout the country.

Lastly, buildings not of, but near, the railway. It is surprising how often there are public houses next to the station, usually the Railway Hotel, reflecting its style, as at Botley, or perhaps shaming it, like that at Eridge. And the railways fed industrial activities and sometimes it is difficult to disentangle one from the other. Sometimes the industrial complexes have a character of their own, such as the cement works at Beeding or at Lewes with their white cliffs made by quarrying, or the Grain oil refinery with its strange shapes in the flat marshes. The sub-stations required by electrification fall into this category perhaps: standard, white, impersonal, and sprouting strange wires, they are essentially Southern.

This is neither a complete survey nor a detailed history of railway architecture in the South-East. It is idiosyncratic: we drew and wrote about what we liked and what interested us, both buildings and smaller structures, and have thus included both the unusual and the ordinary. Whilst no doubt omitting many people's favourites, we hope we shall have introduced them to worthwhile buildings in compensation. We have also dealt with what exists, and a great deal of interest has vanished during the last few years.

DAVID COLE

OUSE VALLEY

The Ouse Valley viaduct of
37 arches, 100ft high, which
carries the Brighton main
line above the green Sussex
pastures, has a grace not
always to be seen in brickwork. This, and the
ornamental parapet and
'pavilions' at each end, are
perhaps to be attributed to
the architect David
Mocatta, a pupil of
Sir John Soane.

16

Clayton Tunnel of 1840, north of Brighton. One of the earliest of a peculiarly British foible — a castellated tunnel mouth, made doubly ridiculous by the cottage on the castle roof and even more anachronistic by the electric train and colour light signal.

SOUTHAMPTON

Sir William Tite's Southampton Terminus of 1840 is given the full classic revival treatment, though the proportions are odd due to the unusual height of the ground floor rooms.

The adjacent building shows the subtle changes in design which the Victorian architects made over the next twenty years. The cornice has lost its dentils and rests on scrolled brackets: the windows are round headed and have large panes of plate glass and the corner pilasters are carefully understated.

POSTAL TELEGRAPHS

SOUTHAMPTON

The unscholarly classical fragments, no doubt
from the 1920's, on this building at Southampton
Docks contrast strangely with the clarity of
Tite's building or the directness of the
adjoining crane. Over the horrid Ocean Liner
Terminal of the 1950's we prefer to draw a veil.

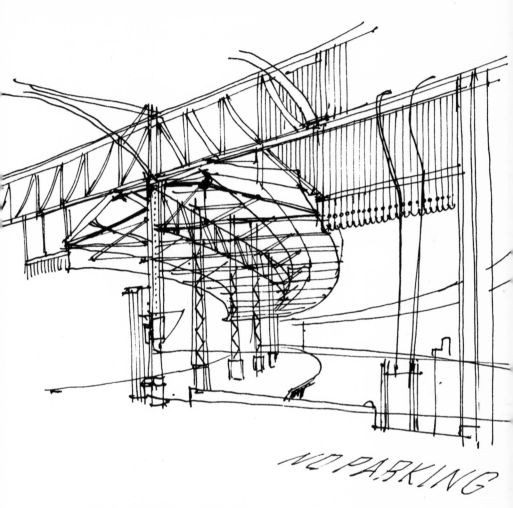

NO PARKING

Inside Southampton Terminus ironwork dashes around in an apparently undisciplined manner. No longer the sweep and breadth of a Brighton, but instead lattice girders run in all directions, even replacing the cast iron columns.

GOSPORT

Gosport was the original Portsmouth terminus of the L&SWR, and the bits of the original building of 1841, a classical edifice carefully detailed remain forgotten in a jungle of foliage. It's tempting to suppose Sir William Tite, who was responsible for the other termini at Nine Elms and Southampton, was here too. The cast iron post box outside is of the same period.

POST

MICHELDEVER

Micheldever station, probably the original
of 1839 but the window heads look wrong,
has classical proportions and dignity,
the road and the platform sides subtly
different, with - a rare thing - canopies
on both sides conceived in the round as
part of the building, and supported on
slim elegant cast-iron columns. The
large plain clock over the entrance door
is a traditional survival reminding us
that watches were once less common
possessions.

MICHELDEVER

The glazed subway roof is but an incident at platform level. Neither this nor the cast iron warning notice prepare us for the monumental character of the subway itself, its sternness relieved only by the scrolls on the roof ties. Such design requires precision in workmanship and scrupulous cleanliness, Just as a building by Mies van der Rohe.

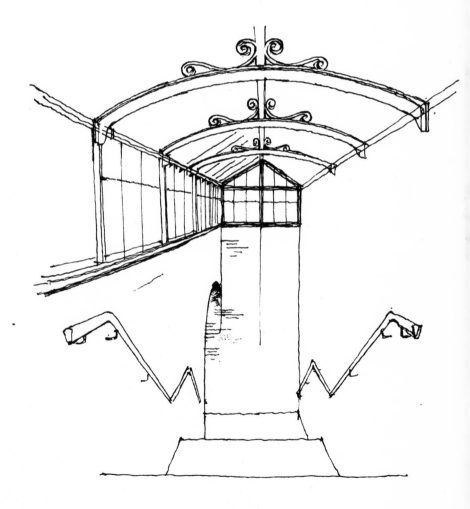

27

BRIGHTON

The original Brighton station was designed by David Mocatta in 1840 in a restrained Classic style. It is still there, totally overpowered by a glass and iron canopy which incidentally is sprouting a louvred lantern, and which serves to emphasise the peculiar levels of the forecourt and road, and by the train shed on the other side.

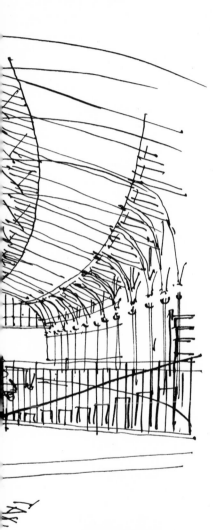

BRIGHTON

The all over roof at Brighton, completed in 1882, is in the mainstream tradition of glass and iron 'train sheds', an international style not confined to Britain.

BRIGHTON

The heavy discoloured and disfigured brickwork of the viaduct over Lewes Road at Brighton has a brooding and sinister appearance so different from the elegance of the Ouse Valley viaduct a few miles to the north. The pilasters ending in cornices are a curious and perhaps not wholly successful attempt to humanise the steam engine with a minimum of classic detail.

YAPTON

Yapton crossing on the LB&SCR coast line near Chichester.
This is probably the 1846 station building, closed in 1864
but in use as staff accommodation. It shows the
immediate post-Mocatta architecture, and looks vaguely
like a toll-house. The level crossing is of the continental
lift-barrier type with flashing lights controlling the
road traffic and obviating the need for the crossing
keeper to live on the spot.

SOLE STREET

The London Chatham & Dover Railway
never had any money, and so some
of its earlier stations, like Sole Street
of 1860, were plain brick villas with
outbuildings and here, surprisingly
prominent chimneys.

FAVERSHAM

~~Faversham~~ station has tall narrow round headed windows lighting the high booking office. These are repeated in the ~~fine~~ brick water tower. The swan necked gas lamps remain.

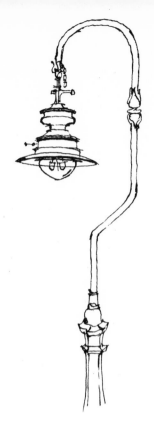

BIRCHINGTON

Birchington on the old LC&DR was opened in 1863 and the slightly Tudor building is a contrast to Sole Street. The up platform awning has been rebuilt without frilly edges and with members cantilevered from columns against the wall, thus obviating the obstruction in the narrow platform. The platform face has been rebuilt with SR pre-cast concrete components. The brick arched road bridge completes a satisfactory composition.

The goods shed, on the other hand, is not Gothic at all: it has a broken pediment and a round louvred opening in the gable.

SELHAM

Selham station, a timber building except
for the fireplaces and chimneys of a type
almost identical, down to the roofless
lavatory in the foreground, except for
minor details with that used on many
country branch lines and very difficult
to date.

MIDHURST

The LB&SCR had a standard type
of very plain cottage rendered a
dingy grey which it built everywhere,
very unlike some examples on other
lines. This pair is at Midhurst

PETWORTH

Petworth Station, a charming timber building gently decaying now that the line is closed and lifted. Contrast this with Selham.

BUXTED

Buxted Viaduct of 1894 rears out of the quiet Wealden countryside like some Roman aqueduct, with its segmental brick arches on solid brick piers.

Buxted station is no doubt the original building of 1868 - a strange mixture of motifs. The canted chimneys were no doubt suggested by sixteenth century houses in the locality: the barge boards are picturesque Gothic: the windows can only be called Victorian. The footbridge of iron lattice construction, looks much better without a roof.

PULBOROUGH

Pulborough on the LBSCR's Mid-
Sussex line, was built about 1860,
at the last gasp of the 'Georgian'
of the early nineteenth century.
The basic elements are there,
the details flattered or coarsened
almost to caricature.
The timber market sale building
on the other hand can only be
described as carpenters' mannerist.
Hundreds of unpretentious buildings
of this kind have disappeared
unrecorded.

BOTLEY

At Botley, a squat signal box of the 1920's in brickwork, partly rendered, contrasts with the tall latticed post with the signal arm duplicated — High, to be seen from a distance. Low, to be seen from nearby.

The Railway Hotel at Botley looks as if it might be a station. The corner pilasters and the windows still retain vestigal traces of Classic revival detail.

PETERSFIELD

The Portsmouth direct line was originally built by the contractor Thomas Brassey, as a speculation in 1855. The station building at Petersfield, perhaps of a slightly later date has the LSWR trick of a single storey with the station house piled up at one end. Here it gives a very strange appearance.

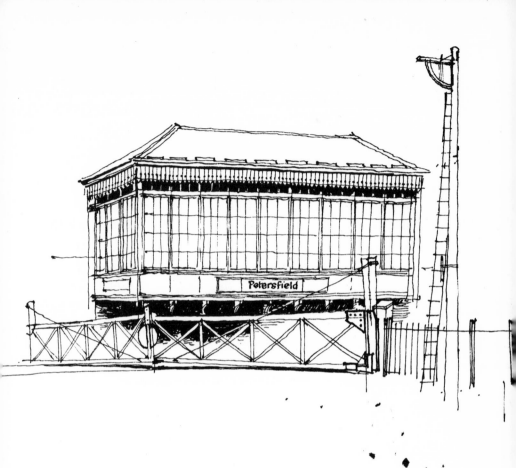

PETERSFIELD

Perhaps the ultimate in signal boxes. A glazed
wall cantilevered out and topped with an
exceptionally small scale canopy edging
assembled as usual from a large number of
standard timber shapes

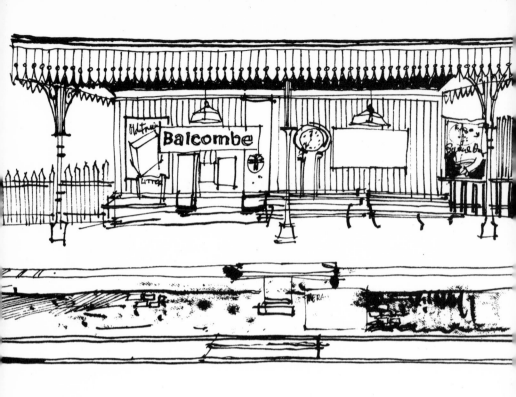

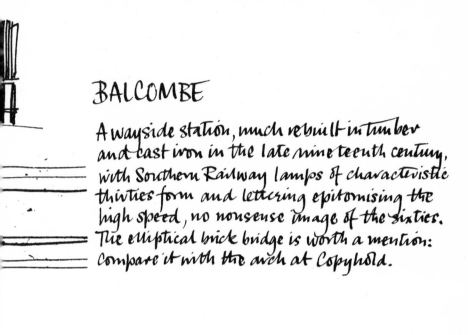

BALCOMBE

A wayside station, much rebuilt in timber
and cast iron in the late nineteenth century,
with Southern Railway lamps of characteristic
thirties form and lettering epitomising the
high speed, no nonsense image of the sixties.
The elliptical brick bridge is worth a mention:
compare it with the arch at Copyhold.

BAYNARDS

Baynards is closed – the track lifted.
The station, a sort of public private
station, is of about 1865 and has
elaborate ridge cresting and chimneys:
it is now occupied as a private house.
Before closure it was remarkable for
its flowers: now dahlias grow in a
green house and the track bed
provides a convenient pit for
car repairs.

BAYNARDS

Precast concrete posts with a pebbled finish
support the name board.
The goods shed still keeps its crane; a
timber post swivels at top and bottom and
supports an arm and brace and simple
mechanism: industrial archaeology for
the children.

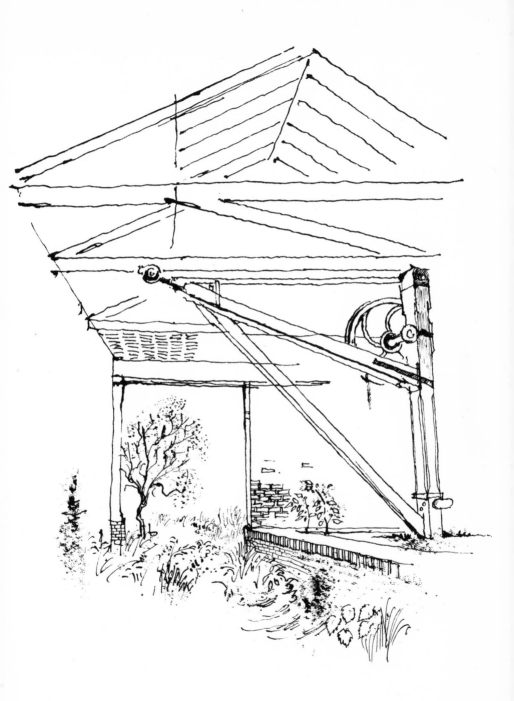

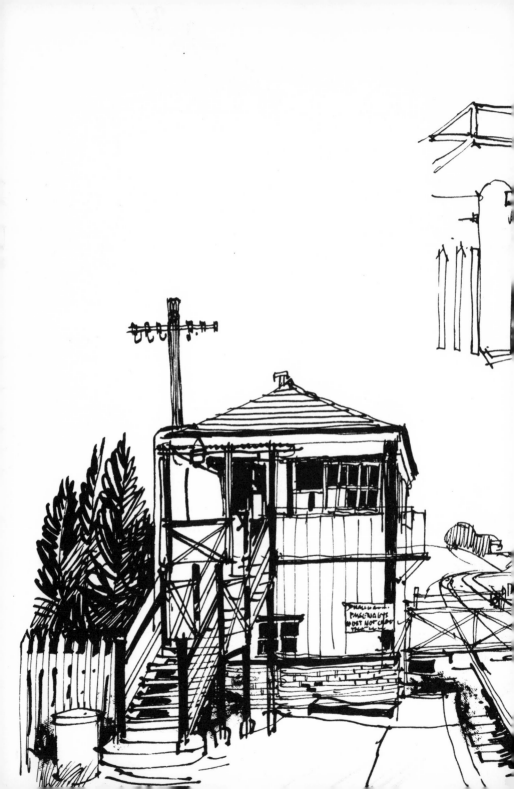

COOKSBRIDGE

The dwarf timber signal box is of an early type, formerly often found standing on high timber legs. This one at Cooksbridge, has a balcony outside the windows, presumably for cleaning purposes

The level crossing gates, of traditional construction, have half-red discs centrally and are hung on massive timber posts and strengthened by a diagonal metal rod.

61

BOXHILL

Boxhill of 1877 (architect C.H. Driver) is a fine example
of a style much used by the former LB&SCR. A tower,
vaguely French, contributes to a picturesquely
varied roof line, whilst all the details, like the
capital, are in a very free Gothic. Here also is the
curved platform awning developed with such
effect at Christs Hospital twenty years later.

BOXHILL

The up platform building at Boxhill has some of the details of a chapel, and the canopy is cantilevered out from the wall on the cast iron brackets.
The station entrance, too, has the look of a church porch.

A dwarf signal by the lineside,
used for shunting purposes and
not designed for sighting at speed

SHEFFIELD PARK

Sheffield Park station of 1882, follows architecturally (though at a distance), the red, tile hung, so called 'Queen Anne' houses which architects like Norman Shaw were building in this area in the 'seventies. Perhaps, as was so often the case, the proximity of a country house after which the station is named encouraged a building of picturesque quality. Now the headquarters of the Bluebell Railway, vintage locomotives, carriages and other material are to be seen here.

LEWES

The new station of 1889, a single storey pavilion
supporting large ball finials and a lantern – a
recurrent LB&SCR motif.

LEWES

This charming cottage, no doubt dating from the 1870's
and whose use is unfathomable, looks as though
it escaped from a Wagnerian stage set. Another
example of Brighton romantic

70

DRIVERS GUARDS
AND SHUNTERS
ARE WARNED
OR HIGH BOX TRUCKS
UNDER THIS BRIDGE

LEWES

The 1889 viaduct at Lewes: the basic bridge, plate girders sitting on brick walls, or on iron columns whose caps are structural. Form follows function, but it does so coarsely.

PAY
HERE
3P FOR 2 HOURS
TICKETS MUST BE
STUCK ON INSIDE
OF WINDSCREEN

LEWES

Railways serve industry, and run into the factories and installations. Lewes is dominated by a great chalk cliff the product of quarrying and the cement works at the foot of the cliff is rail served.

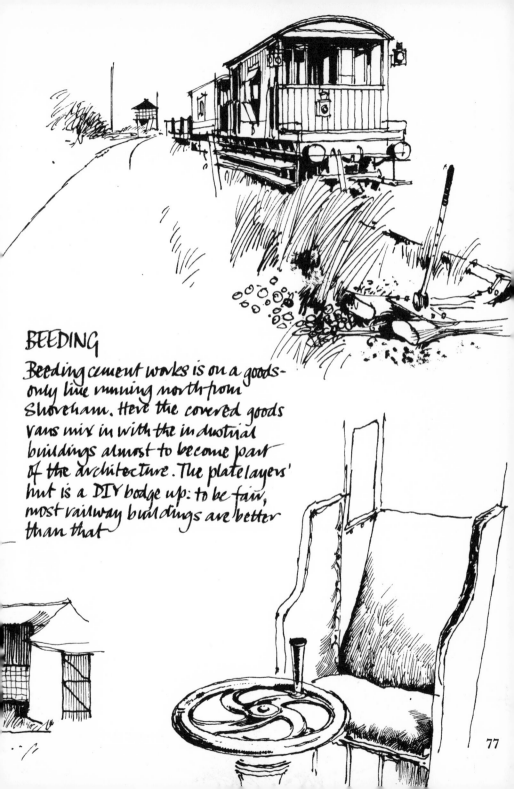

BEEDING

Beeding cement works is on a goods-
only line running north from
Shoreham. Here the covered goods
vans mix in with the industrial
buildings almost to become part
of the architecture. The platelayers'
hut is a DIY bodge up: to be fair,
most railway buildings are better
than that

77

WROTHAM

The red brick Gothic style station is a pattern which constantly recurs: this typical example is Wrotham and Borough Green. The heavy double hung sash windows with plate glass and pointed arches are in the true Gilbert Scott tradition.

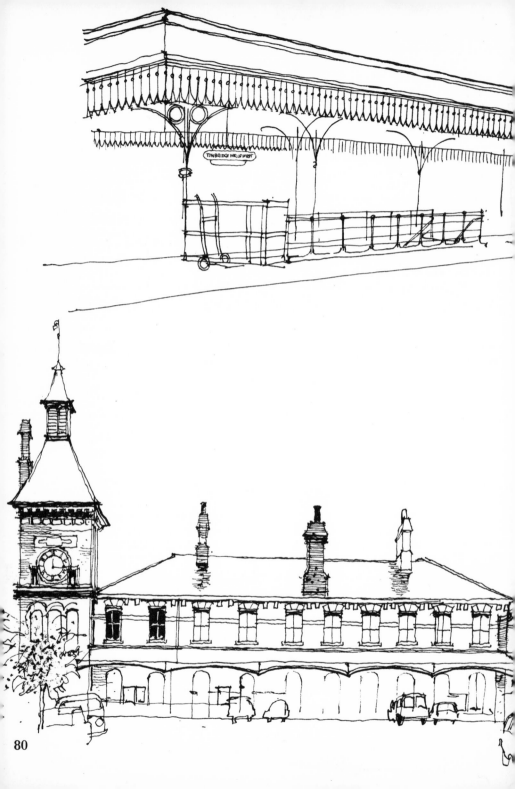

TUNBRIDGE WELLS WEST

TUNBRIDGE WELLS WEST

Tunbridge Wells West was the terminus for most of the LB&SCR trains using it, and the station of the early 1880's has survived as a late Victorian period piece. Note the engineer's stripped Gothic detail the emphatic clock tower, the chimneys after Butterfield, one growing unhappily out of the tower, the canopy on the roadside giving on to an enormous forecourt (an LB&SCR foible), and the use of timber whether in the usual glass, iron and wood platform awnings with the standard restless edge, or in the immense louvred clerestory which the gentlemen's loo sports.

TUNBRIDGE WELLS WEST

A perverse and ornate little timber porch is
tacked on to one side of the tower at Tunbridge
Wells West, apparently because a staircase
turned out to be longer than expected
A painted wooden board exhorts the defunct
steam engine to whistle in case of passengers
waiting at the also defunct High Rocks Halt.
It is flanked by a standard SR precast
concrete gradient post, indicating a change,
with metal figures fixed into it: and by a
standard SR precast post and panel platelayers' hut, with, however the brick chimney
surviving from an earlier period.

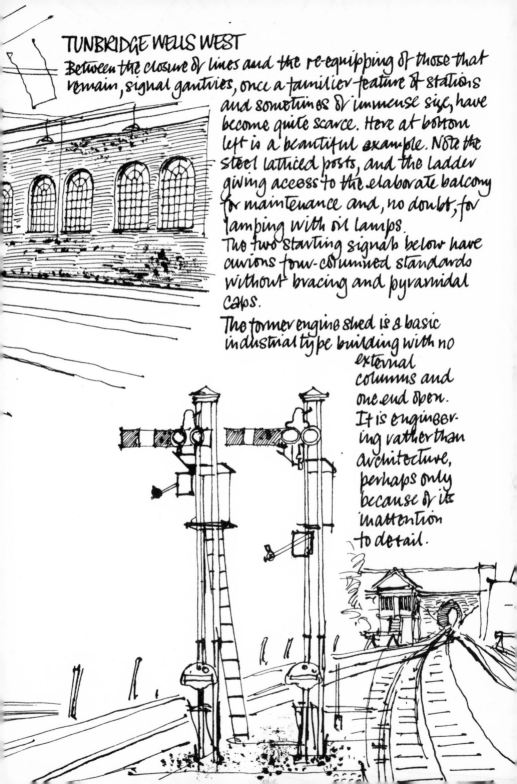

TUNBRIDGE WELLS WEST

Between the closure of lines and the re-equipping of those that remain, signal gantries, once a familiar feature of stations and sometimes of immense size, have become quite scarce. Here at bottom left is a beautiful example. Note the steel latticed posts, and the ladder giving access to the elaborate balcony for maintenance and, no doubt, for lamping with oil lamps.

The two starting signals below have curious four-columned standards without bracing and pyramidal caps.

The former engine shed is a basic industrial type building with no external columns and one end open. It is engineering rather than architecture, perhaps only because of its inattention to detail.

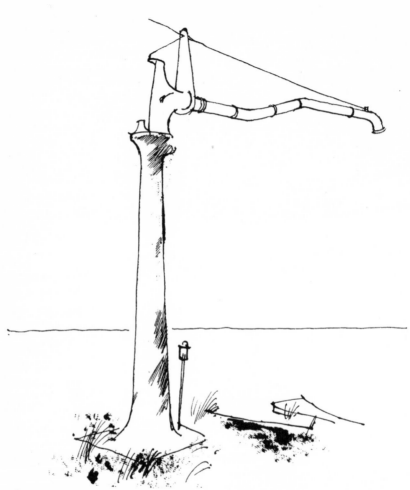

TUNBRIDGE WELLS WEST

Steam locomotives required water: storage tanks for
the water came in many different kinds. That at
Tunbridge Wells West remains — a very basic structure,
a riveted iron cistern with a lid on eight tall
tubular iron columns. The water is fed into a crane —
a hollow cast iron column with a swivel arm and
a flexible hose at its end. This one has lost its
hose and the iron wheel which operated the tap.

ENQUIRIES PARCELS
AND LEFT LUGGAGE

Diary of Event

TUNBRIDGE WELLS WEST

Above: the station booking office.
Right: the curious spidery light
standard is again precast
concrete of the SR. From it hang
gas lamps which are still in use.

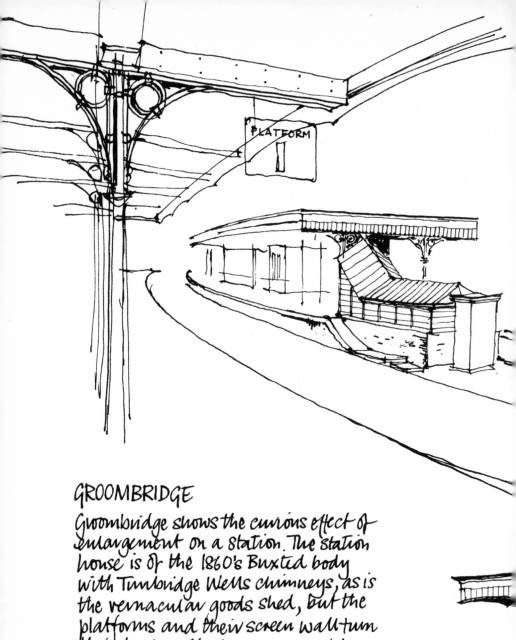

PLATFORM

GROOMBRIDGE

Groombridge shows the curious effect of
enlargement on a station. The station
house is of the 1860's Buxted body
with Tunbridge Wells chimneys, as is
the vernacular goods shed, but the
platforms and their screen wall turn
their back on the house very rudely.

BRITISH RAILWAYS
NOTICE

THIS BRIDGE IS INSUFFICIENT
TO CARRY ANY VEHICLE
THE WEIGHT OF ANY AXLE OF
WHICH EXCEEDS 2 TONS

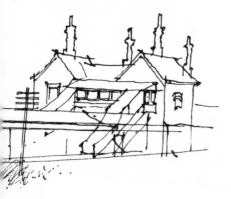

ERIDGE

Eridge is a country junction where two very long timber buildings crowned with the usual iron and wood roofs (now with corrugated asbestos in place of most of the glass) and with prominent brick chimneys, rear improbably out of the flat fields. In steam days the trains exchanged coaches with each other to a remarkable degree.

The timber occupation bridge bears a notice pointing out its light construction.

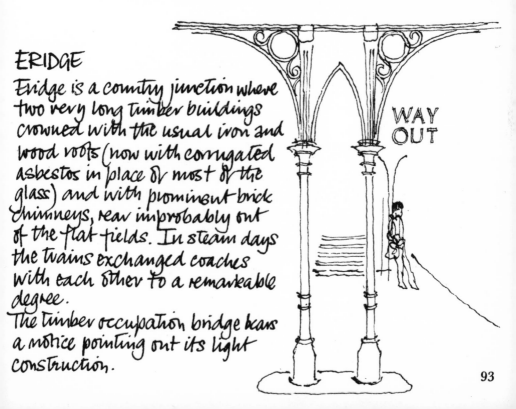

WAY
OUT

93

ERIDGE

The vernacular architecture takes its tone from the buildings on the Eridge Estate, in a recognisable style originated by J. Montier in 1810-30: this lodge opposite the station is nicely complemented by the erstwhile 'Railway Hotel' adjoining the station.

ERIDGE

The railways' buildings make an effort to keep in keeping, with somewhat Emett like results as at ~~Forge Farm~~ occupation crossing near Eridge.

Above is Eridge station, viewed from the lifted Heathfield Line. The effort has been all too much, and the mean LB&SCR cottage is again on the ascendant.

97

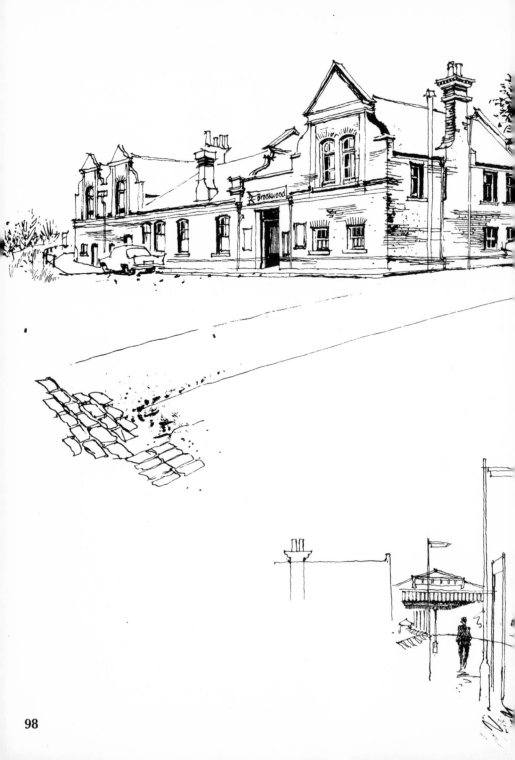

BROOKWOOD

Brookwood station was rebuilt some time shortly after 1900, and the prominent red brick gables come from Holland through seventeenth century England through Norman Shaw through speculative South London builders, whence the civil engineer has appropriated them to adorn his elevation with less than happy results. The platform awnings here are, rather unusually, hipped at the ends. The inside is wide open, more like a continental than an English station.

Brookwood

WEST MEON

The Alton to Winchester line was a very late comer. Open in 1902 and with engineering works on a massive scale for Hampshire, it never attained importance and is now closed. The stations were massive too. Here is West Meon, which might be a small country house after the style of Sir Guy Dawber or Baillie Scott, but for the unusual sliding doors opening on to the platform, the better no doubt to handle parcels traffic.

CHRISTS HOSPITAL

Christs Hospital station was opened in 1902 when the school had moved nearby from London. It is at the junction with the Shoreham and the Guildford line, both, alas, closed. The house itself, an undistinguished effort in polychrome brickwork, contrasts with the water tower, the engineer had to build a brick base to prop up a metal tank and he did just that.

The Christs Hospital boys arriving at the beginning of term wear an anachronistic blue uniform.

CHRISTS HOSPITAL

The station house at Christs Hospital contrasts still
more strikingly with the platform shelters where
the heavy timber panels, cross braced and boarded,
and the cast iron columns, support timber and
glass roofs from which depend ornamental canopies
with splendid sweeping curves so unlike the
continuously repeated spikes of Balcombe, adding
up to a work of art of exceptional quality in no
known style.
Note the signal: a semaphore arm in a lighted
panel. A warning, and an indication where to
stop addressed to drivers of six coach trains.

LOAD NOT TO EXCEED 1 TON 18CWT

CHRISTS HOSPITAL

A goods shed is a building of a decided character: doorways in the ends for trucks to enter, a platform inside, a simple crane, a side loading bay with tall doors and a canopy for road vehicles, and an office, perhaps, as here, tacked on and having in its details some regard to local traditional construction.

CROWBOROUGH

The LBSCR's Tunbridge Wells to Brighton line was
doubled through Crowborough about 1894, and
the new station clearly dates from thereabouts,
at a time when country house architects like
Baillie Scott were active in the locality. It
should be possible to fit an architect's name to
this: it is a cut above most other stations of its
type. Materials – hard dark red brick (not the
local product) below tiling – and details have
alike been carefully considered. It can well
be appreciated across a forecourt large as a
barrack square.

The signal box is a fine example of the common
timber glazed top on brick base.

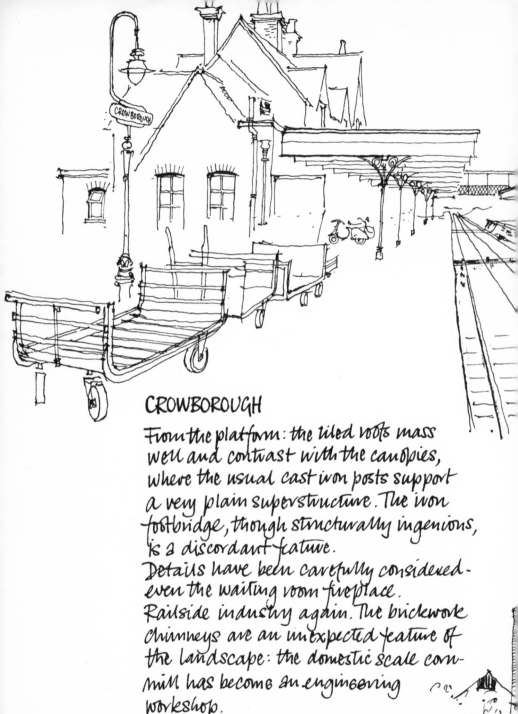

CROWBOROUGH

From the platform: the tiled roofs mass
well and contrast with the canopies,
where the usual cast iron posts support
a very plain superstructure. The iron
footbridge, though structurally ingenious,
is a discordant feature.

Details have been carefully considered -
even the waiting room fireplace.

Railside industry again. The brickwork
chimneys are an unexpected feature of
the landscape: the domestic scale corn-
mill has become an engineering
workshop.

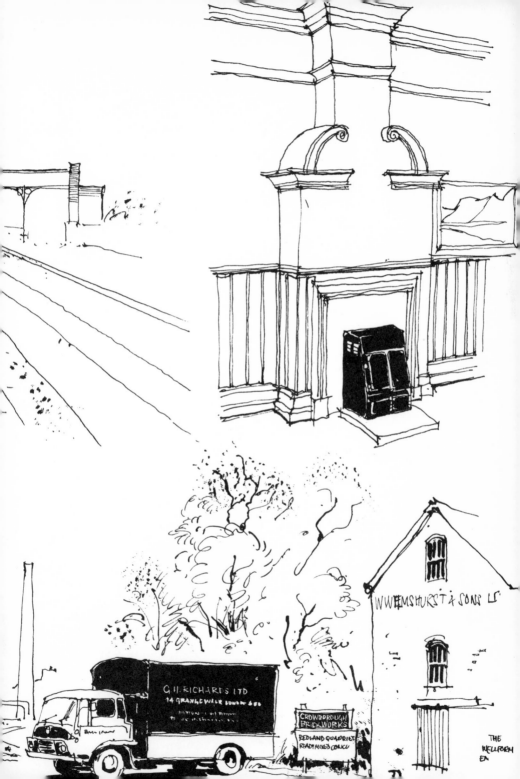

G H RICHARDS LTD
14 GRANGE WALK BOUGH 580

CROWBOROUGH
BRICKWORKS

REDLAND QUARRIES
READY MIXED CONCU

W WEEMSHURST & SONS L^T

THE
WELLFORM
EN

UCKFIELD

Uckfield was built at the same time as Crowborough, but manifestly designed by a lesser hand. It has the clichés of the time — a Voysey gable sweeping down, or a little Baillie Scott half timbering. The overbridge too is curiously amorphous.

ARUNDEL

This goods shed is rewarding - the lunettes and brick panels nicely handled, whilst it is unusually of two storeys.

WORTING JUNCTION

At Worting junction in Hampshire the lattice girder bridge, rearing strangely out of the fields, carries one line over another so that the Southampton and West of England trains do not delay each other. Each bridge carries a number: 143A indicates this was an afterthought.

PENSHURST

Penshurst is Janus. The village of Chiddingstone Causeway was much rebuilt in a characterful sixteenth century revival by the architect George Devey in the 1870's. One side of the station takes its line from Devey, although it is now obscured by piles of timber: the other, facing the platform, is genteel neo-Georgian of the twenties sadly marred by the blocking up of all the windows of this unstaffed halt against vandals.

The signal box is on the other hand very normal. The staggered platforms were a common feature on the old SER.

TUNBRIDGE WELLS CENTRAL

Tunbridge Wells Central is schizo-
phrenic. A rich deep brown post-
1923 station building with
strangely effective free Classic
detail and a charming tower
(who was the architect?) leads
into narrow dark platforms
between two tunnels where
it seems always to be evening.
The original building of 1845
in a different 'free Classic'
remains on the up side.

British Rail Tunbridge Wells Central

Tickets
Information
Left Luggage

DUMPTON PARK

The London Chatham and Dover Railway went everywhere
the South Eastern went, and both lines served both
Ramsgate and Margate, on the Kent Coast, in a highly
inconvenient manner. One of the first things the Southern
Railway did was to rationalise these lines, and a
product of this was the new station of Dumpton Park at
Ramsgate, built in 1926. Presumably designed by an
engineering trainee, its architecture
defies description. Why ever, for instance,
place a tea-cosy on top of an iron
section out of a pier to make
a cupola? The footbridge
leading to the platforms has
iron roof trusses of a
splendidly old-fashioned
appearance.

HAYWARDS HEATH

A contrast in bridges on the London
to Brighton main line: right, at
Haywards Heath where electrification and increased traffic has
caused rebuilding, and above at
Copyhold, not far north, where the
brick archway has, about 1864,
had abutments added to take
a line which was never built.

HAYWARDS HEATH

Haywards Heath is a town created by the railway.
The station has been entirely rebuilt by the Southern
Railway in connexion with the electrification of
the London to Brighton main line in 1932. Notice
the modern platform awning, with a plain eaves
in place of the earlier fretted and ornamented
timber members, and the plate girder bridge

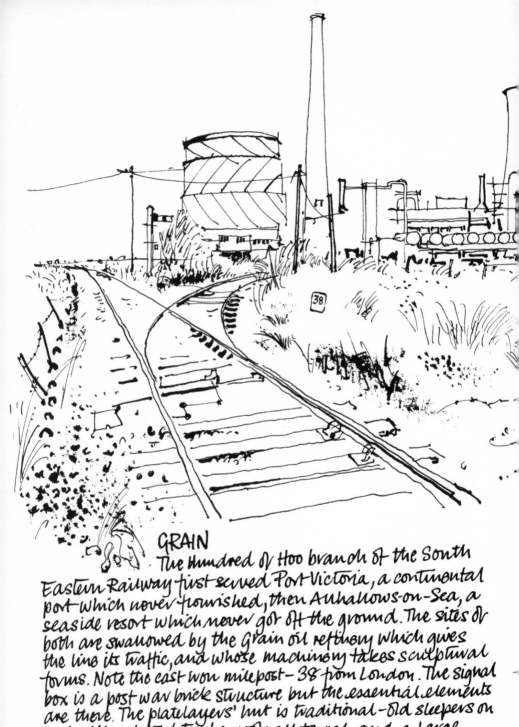

GRAIN

The Hundred of Hoo branch of the South Eastern Railway first served Port Victoria, a continental port which never flourished, then Allhallows-on-Sea, a seaside resort which never got off the ground. The sites of both are swallowed by the Grain oil refinery which gives the line its traffic, and whose machinery takes sculptural forms. Note the cast iron milepost — 38 from London. The signal box is a post war brick structure but the essential elements are there. The platelayers' hut is traditional — old sleepers on end with a felted timber roof, all tarred, and a large brick fireplace.

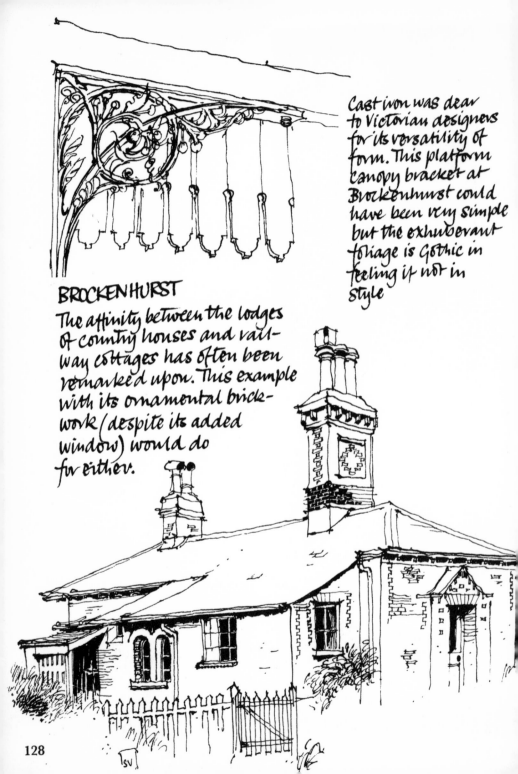

Cast iron was dear to Victorian designers for its versatility of form. This platform canopy bracket at Brockenhurst could have been very simple but the exhuberant foliage is Gothic in feeling if not in style

BROCKENHURST

The affinity between the lodges of country houses and railway cottages has often been remarked upon. This example with its ornamental brickwork (despite its added window) would do for either.